Where Fear Meets Faith

Heartfelt Stories of Connection, Surviving Cancer, & Living Life

Tina Calderone Roth

www.wherefearmeetsfaith.com

Where Fear Meets Faith/ Tina Calderone-Roth. -- 1st ed.
ISBN 979-8-234-05004-5

To my daughter Sarah, I am graced to be your mother. You are my inspiration for life and love. I am so proud of you. To my husband Gary, you are a tower of strength for me. To my father Jim for giving me the gift of heart and the early understanding of human connection.

"Every time you smile at someone, it is an action of love,
a gift to that person,
a beautiful thing."

--- Mother Teresa

Contents

WELCOME

I would like to warmly welcome you to this tapestry of personal stories about surviving cancer and challenging life events. These are my own stories of vulnerability, encouragement, faith, connection, and love. As my journey unfolded, I began to notice incredible moments of meaning and compassion happening all around me, every single day. I felt a deep need to somehow capture this new-found sense of connection, even though I wasn't sure how to do that at first. Then, one day, it began with just a single story.

In 2022, I received a cancer diagnosis that changed the rhythm of our home in ways we could never have imagined. Life suddenly felt unfamiliar, and each of us found ourselves navigating moments of uncertainty and fear that were deeper than anything we had known. There were days when the weight of the unknown felt overwhelming; and yet, even in the midst of those difficult moments, something beautiful began to unfold. We discovered tender expressions of love, quiet acts of courage, and meaningful connections that gently reminded us we were not alone. Through the darkness, there were also moments of light—moments that revealed the strength of the human spirit and the faith that can carry us through even the most challenging seasons.

I came to realize that I had gathered a collection of moments centered around our family and friends lifting each other up and deeply rooted in human connection. There were such powerful and moving experiences taking place. The unfortunate part I noticed was that many of these stories often went unspoken. I genuinely believe that even the smallest act of kindness has the power to change a life, and I am here to share that for me, this could not be truer.

The stories that follow reflect meaningful moments from my life. They are not chronological order, but more in an order of Family, Gratitude, Healing, and Legacy. In these moments, I learned how important it is to recognize that even the simplest gestures can leave a lasting imprint on the heart. Each story is meant to be a brief glimpse into times that were truly special and deeply personal.

At the end of each story, I offer questions to encourage reflection, gratitude and positivity. I hope you enjoy these stories and that they bring you comfort, inspiration, and a sense of connection.

PART ONE

Family: The Love That Carried Us Through

Petals Between Us: A Mother, A Daughter, and a Garden of Time

After having a baby girl, getting into the groove of driving on my own with her in the car seat made me nervous. I would stick around my local area and would not venture out too far. One day, which I still remember as if it was yesterday, we went for a drive. It was a cool October morning during the week. The sky was overcast and it was slightly grey.

I dressed my two-month-old daughter in a pretty floral dress and loaded up the car with the stroller and enough baby care items to last for days, even though I was going to be out for a couple of hours. We drove to the LA Arboretum, which was several cities away. When we arrived, I could feel this incredible positive and magical energy in the air. I bundled up my daughter, placed her in her stroller, and off we went walking amongst gorgeous floral gardens, stunning trees, and a hand full of passersby. Each person there was so kind and greeted each other with warm pleasantries.

We listened to the soft breeze, the chirping of birds and watched the squirrels hop by. Also, there were pretty peacocks and peahens just meandering around. It was so peaceful and renewing to be surrounded by such beauty. The air was crisp and there was a sweet mist in the air. It was like a fine delicate veil that surrounded us. This brought out such calming scents of lavender.

At one point we came across this large shell. It was half of a giant clam shell. It was propped up as if it was ready to hold something. Instantly, I had an idea. I picked up my daughter with her soft pastel blankets, and I placed her in the shell. She looked as if she was the birth of Venus. So peaceful and sweet. I quickly snapped a photo. She was at peace there; the photo was completed in the blink of an eye, but what happened after has lasted a lifetime.

That photo has been shared with many and still brings so much joy to our family and friends. It captures such tranquil, peaceful and loving energy. The following year I remembered that it was the same time that we went on that road trip. We had to return to that special place, and I recaptured the photo in the shell; but this time, my daughter no longer fit in the shell since she had grown so much in her first year.

This became a sweet tradition for my daughter and I. We made the trip there every year and stood next to the shell to mark this special time for us and to also show how much she has grown. Fourteen years have gone by and the tradition continues. We love this time together, reflecting on the past years, making plans for future visits, and wondering how long the shell will remain there. Although the shell is an object, it has become a special friend for my daughter and I.

It is so important to take time to pause, reflect and be at peace. Time is moving so quickly. Let's do what we can to capture the special moments and genuinely enjoy them. It is only these 'things' that can be taken with us as our journey continues. This is something I learned as I faced challenging times going through cancer. This story I would treasure and reflect upon when I was receiving treatment, because I wanted in my heart to not miss a year of our beloved tradition.

Is there a special place that brings you comfort, joy, and fond memories? Are there any new places where you could create new memories or traditions with your loved ones?

A Sisterhood Through Cancer: I Was Lifted Up

Being the only child in a family that was much older had its challenges. Normally, people would say things like: “Oh, being the only child, you must be spoiled”. This could not be further from the truth. As the only child, I had to live up to high expectations. Many of my relatives were much older and relating to older generations was just different from having a young sibling around to connect with.

I had always longed to have siblings, but instead I was home alone most of the time. As I grew up, I developed real friendships that have lasted me a lifetime, and I have been forever blessed. It is because of these friendships that I am here today. I have strong bonds with these friends that now transcend to my husband and my daughter.

From middle school, high school, college, previous jobs, and community programs, I have been surrounded by incredible humans. We stay connected all sorts of ways. Social media, car rides, flights, dinners, letters and wonderful conversations. There is spirit in these relationships that mere words are not able to capture.

As life leads us through twists, and turns, it is these friends who have been there with me when I was not certain of what the next day would bring. We shared many tears and so much laughter. Special handmade mementos to capture certain events in our lives, beautiful cards, and hugs I will treasure always.

My little family has been hit with a difficult diagnosis for my daughter and a cancer diagnosis for myself. To make matters worse, they occurred during the same time. It was like the wind was knocked right out of us. Not knowing if we would make it to the next day, was extremely difficult for us on so many levels.

My friendships were not just important for me; these incredible friends were there for my husband and my daughter when we needed a lifeline. When I was going through chemotherapy and multiple surgeries, it was these very friends that were creating food trains, lifting us up in prayer, running errands, watching my daughter when I could not, checking in on all of us, and many pilgrimages on our behalf.

Just recently, I have faithful friends who, without hesitation, crawled through mud along with me to show support and solidarity for cancer survival. I did not even need to ask; they willingly volunteered to be waist deep in mud. I trust these friends with my life, and they are always in my heart.

I have close friends who have become more than just friends, they have truly become my family. I know that I would not be here today without the love, support and encouragement from these very special people in my life. I do believe in a higher power and that these individuals were put in my life for a reason. Never underestimate the power, connection, and love of true friendships.

I know that I am never alone.

What friendships have left a lasting impact in your life? What act of kindness can you share with someone in your life?

A Husband Staying Brave: When Shaken by the Unknown

On an early spring day, I had to make a phone call to my husband: a phone call that no wife wants to make. I had to tell my husband, Gary, that I was in the ER and that they had found a tumor. I was frightened, but I didn't want to pass this fear on to him. Gary asked where I was and stated that he would be there right away.

More than anything, I wanted and needed him there with me, however we needed help because our ten-year-old daughter, Sarah, would be getting out of school and there was no one to pick her up and to stay with her. We needed to figure things out. I asked him to please be there for Sarah, and I could hear a quiver in his voice because he knew that he couldn't be in two cities at the same time. I can't even begin to imagine how difficult that must have been for him. We are a small family, and we have our schedules and childcare down to a science to make sure everything is covered.

The problem was, everything was not covered, and we didn't have a contingency plan. We were in new territory, and we did not know what lay ahead. There were several times during my medical journey that my husband had to somehow be in multiple places at once. And ... He was.

Being a protector, provider, father, husband, and making sure everyone was safe, was something he would do. But this time, everything was out of our control. I ended up having a minor procedure that day and eventually drove myself home. We spoke on the phone until I made it home. We sat together and cried. All we did was sit there together in silence. The shock was just so overwhelming for us in that moment.

For five surgeries, infusions, and post-surgical appointments, Gary was there to be a father to a child who really needed him during the uncertainty. He was also there trying to make sure I was safe. Cancer is not something anyone wants, but in our case, we learned to function together and make it through. Gary was there to help move my shabby chic vanity table and mirror outside in the driveway. I asked him to do this for me, and he was not sure why, but he did it anyway. This happened the day I realized that I needed to shave my head because my hair was falling out in clumps. Together we supported our daughter through this change. We each took part and shaved my head. Tears, tears and more tears.

The most special moment came after, when my husband shaved his head to support me. There is a photo of him kissing my bald head. We made it through that moment together. This would not be the last of the fearful moments, but it was the togetherness that carried us through.

I often look back upon this time we experienced, and I reflect on Gary just trying to take care of our family and push through the fear to get through to the other side. Things were not pretty. Actually, they were quite messy. But we made it through together.

Who has been that constant support presence in your life? How have they enriched your life?

Love, Resilience and a Wagging Tail

The interesting thing about chemotherapy is that its side effects are unique to each individual. However, one common side effect is fatigue. Personally, each round of treatment brought its own set of changes, progress, challenges, and side effects. I found that each cycle required its own adjustments.

It can be misleading to think that after completing one round of chemotherapy, you are prepared for the next. I quickly discovered that this was not the case. Each round was different, and that uncertainty genuinely concerned me. I am a planner, but there was no plan. You just have to go with it. As treatment progressed, I noticed changes in my strength, endurance, coordination, and memory. Each of these aspects seemed to shift, sometimes unexpectedly, thus making the journey all the more challenging.

The Comfort of Zoe and Unconditional Love

One of the most helpful parts of my recovery was our family dog, Zoe. She was a 16 1/2-year-old miniature pinscher and chihuahua mix. She had been a loving presence in our family, acting as a little momma to our daughter when she was born. Zoe played a significant role in our lives, and we often say that she taught us how to be parents and family.

After returning home from my treatment, I would rest, and Zoe would lie right next to me. She would position herself alongside my hip, looking at me and placing her paw on me to offer comfort. Her presence brought me a sense of peace and reassurance. I could sense her concern and worry whenever I moved or tried to get up. Zoe watched attentively to ensure I was all right. On occasions when I moaned or cried, she would run to get my husband to check on me.

I often talked to Zoe, and we would hold our heads together, as if to share a deeper understanding and connecting of our mind's eye. The connection we shared was truly special and brought me immense comfort during my recovery.

Preparing for Goodbye

As Zoe grew older, I would hold her and gently tell her that when her time came, I needed her to give me a sign. I promised to make sure she was safe, comfortable, and surrounded by family. The thought of having to put an animal down was difficult, but I knew that if her quality of life ever became an issue, we would address it together as a family and with grace.

Two years after recovery from my cancer, we noticed that Zoe herself was slowing down. She was getting older, and she outlived her siblings Bailey and Montgomery. She would sit and rest more. She wrapped herself up in warm fuzzy blankets. We would laugh because she had soft little beds in each room in the house. She had cozy sweaters to keep her warm and pillows to rest her head.

At one point, we had to keep changing her food, as she was not able to eat regular dog food. We started cooking for her, pureeing her food, and spoon feeding her. We knew the end was coming, but she just kept going. She did not express any issue with pain, but she was slowing down. I talked with her, held her, and asked for a sign.

One morning, I was not able to sleep well, so I went to the family room to watch documentaries on TV. Zoe jumped up on the sofa next to me and looked right at me and then jumped back down on the floor. She walked away. I could see that she was restless. She went outside. I went out to bring her in as it was a cold January morning. I wrapped her up in one of her blankets and she rested on the sofa.

A few minutes later she jumped down on the floor and collapsed. My eyes were full of tears. This was it. She was fading away right in front of me. I held her and praised her for being such an incredible part of our family. It was my turn to support her and show her my love for her during this time of transition.

Death is a part of life. Having experienced many deaths in my field of social work, I wanted to ensure this experience be special for Zoe, but also to teach my young daughter about death, dying and how to honor the memory of loved ones. I gathered the family.

There we were as a family kneeling around Zoe on the floor. We will never forget how much love she gave us.

We love you Zoe, aka "little mamas".

What are the ways you honor your loving family pets? Do you share stories or glance over photos? What are ways you keep their memory alive?

Cherished Moments at the Waterfront

As a mom, I have learned that being a mother is the most important role that I will ever have in my life. Seeing your child grow, learn, and become their own person is an amazing gift. Time is moving so quickly, and my daughter is growing into an independent young lady. Having realized that she will be on her own path eventually, I want to cherish every moment and to ensure long lasting memories for us as a family.

About 6 years ago, we started taking “mommy & me” road trips to nearby areas. We realized how important it was for us to have adventures, learn about life, and create lasting memories. We would jump in the car and go for a ride to see various places, meet new people, experience art and culture.

To this day, we continue to talk about the experiences we had during our past adventures.

One such drive became one of our most treasured times, so much so that we would return to one special place often; a sweet trip on the California 101 Highway was just a joy. Driving out of the city and spending time in Ventura at the beach, shopping in the antique stores and visiting the mission were all memorable times for us.

On one trip to Ventura, we had no real plans and so we decided to drive a little longer and we ended up in Santa Barbara. We had been there before, but this time we decided to stop in the small local eateries and shops. We drove onto Stearns Wharf; it was an experience driving on the wharf and hearing the sound of the wood planks when you crossed over with each tire. We laughed as we looked at the GPS screen to see that our car looked like it was in the ocean. We even took a screen shot of the map to remember that moment because it was so funny to us.

We walked around and bought a scoop of ice cream. After, we then sat on this one special bench to look out into the sea. The sun shined down on us. The birds singing all around us. The cool breeze embraced us.

We sat and talked about dreams, goals, and growing up. I shared with my daughter that I would always be around if she wanted to talk, ask for advice or even just toss ideas around. It meant the world to me that she understood that she knew her voice mattered & that she could always ask questions and share ideas. We sat there and just talked about anything and everything. It was a moment of connection that we both remember and treasure.

It is the simple moments that can have the most impact. I sometimes will sit and reflect on that day, and I can feel sun and hear my daughter's laughter. When going through treatment, I would look over the photos from this place and they lifted me up. We have since returned to this place multiple times and it never gets old. We have learned that having these times together helps each of us as individuals, and as mother and daughter.

What special plan or tradition has had a lasting impact on you and your family? Will you pass this on to future generations?

Safe Haven: Returning to the Creek Where My Grief Was Laid to Rest

At the tender age of 2 ½, my father and I stayed with my aunt and her family in her beautiful southern home nestled in a peaceful part of Ooltewah Tennessee. Her home was a place of refuge and love for us during difficult family times. Her home was a safe haven from turmoil. On her acreage, she had a small creek that ran the length of her property. I would play there, dip my feet into the cool, tranquil waters, and listen to the sweet babbling sounds. I knew in my head and in my heart that I was safe.

My father must have known in his heart that we would be supported and cared for at this place. He had to make the tough decision to find a home for me. I cannot imagine how difficult that would have been for young single father so many years ago.

Later in my life, my father's life was cut short, and he passed away before questions could be answered and without any means of closure for me. The last time I saw him was at my graduation from high school. I had a lifetime journey of working through his passing and not having him in my life for very long.

I eventually got married. As one can imagine, the day of the wedding was emotional not having my father there to give me away. However, I felt his spirit there with me the entire time. His favorite color of purple was proudly represented in the theme of the wedding, in his honor. As my husband and I were on our way to our honeymoon, something so magical happened. We were driving along and I was gazing out the passenger side window and wishing that my dad could have been there at the wedding. I was wondering if he would be proud of what I had achieved, my schooling, my career, and my husband. As we were in an area that really did not have good radio connection, clear as day, "Operator" by Jim Croce came on the one station we could get. I instantly burst into tears. This was my father's favorite singer. We would spend years singing his songs in the car. I received this as a sign from my father. My heart was beaming.

I have always longed to return to my aunt's home in Ooltewah, but life got in the way: further family complexities, and a cancer diagnosis prevented me from returning. I shared my special memories of my aunt and her home with my daughter, Sarah, for many years & dreamt about bringing her to my aunt's home. Time did not permit this to happen. However, after clearance from our doctors, we now had the opportunity for me to bring Sarah to this place I held so dearly in my heart. Being able to show her around and seeing her experience the tranquility brought me so much joy. As I stood in the middle of the beautiful trees, historic home and the creek, it was like two worlds had sweetly collided. I was back there as a child but at the same time I was present as a mother with my daughter. I was weak in my knees. This would be the closest we could get for my Sarah to be where her grandfather lived long before she was born. All the pain, sadness, and fear were washed away and now we were left with pure joy.

I stood there and turned in full circles to take in every angle. I closed my eyes and listened to wind blowing in the beautiful trees. I wanted to capture every moment, every scent and every sound so that I could reflect upon it when I returned home. It was like a Garden of Eden. My heart was so overjoyed that I got to share this experience with my daughter. It was like my father was there, and I could spend time with the both of them in two different worlds all at once. Little did I know that this experience with my Sarah would bring closure to a lot of sadness and pain and bring me back to the present day a stronger person. I am now more confident, and able to take steps to grow.

We all experience sadness in our families. However, I believe in my heart that sadness can turn to joy & peace if we are able to pause and reflect on all that is around us.

I have so much to be grateful for.

What challenging memory can you view in a different light? What are the things you need for closure?

Rise Up Warrior

At the cancer center where I received my care and treatment there is a rock garden. It has become a very special place for me and for many others. It is a meditation pathway filled with beautiful river rocks and bamboo plants. Also, present is a grand and awe-inspiring statue that I never really knew the title of or its meaning. All I knew was that its presence commanded strength and resilience.

On the last day of my chemotherapy, I wanted to celebrate, not just for myself, I wanted to celebrate for all who went through the journey alongside me. It was a celebration for us all. To commemorate this time, my family, friends, coworkers, and my incredible oncologist came together to RING THE BELL. We created a parade cheering with colors of teal to represent and honor those fighting ovarian cancer. During the parade, we played “Gonna Fly Now” by Bill Conte, best known as Rocky’s

Theme song. I rang the bell to mark the completion of six rounds of chemotherapy.

It was a very powerful and meaningful time surrounded by everyone. We took lots of photos and really enjoyed time together. Cheers, tears, and hugs were so impactful, especially coming out of pandemic time. It's a day that I will always cherish and something that we all completed together. It wasn't just me. We all crossed the finish line together.

For some reason that rock garden had always been so moving to me, even before my celebration there. You can just feel the energy there that I cannot explain. Every year I go back there, and I spend time reflecting and giving thanks. I have embarked on an ongoing project from the heart. I gather folks to paint positive messages on rocks, and we leave them in the in this rock garden. I have been doing this for about five years, even before my diagnosis. I've scheduled events called Positivity Rocks. We get together and paint rocks for the garden. When you walk among the garden, you see all these colors, beautiful colors, and the most special messages of positivity and other rocks in honor of those who have gone before us. It's such an uplifting experience to see how special this place has become. The intention is to put love, faith, and positivity into the artwork on the rocks and to leave them there in the garden in hopes that someone will pick one up. If a person is having a difficult time, they can pick up a rock that speaks to them and take it with them. The intention is that the energy put into each rock art will transcend onto the recipient.

One weekend, my daughter and I took another batch of rocks over to the rock garden. We stood and gazed at the statue there. It's very abstract and I never really knew what the meaning was. I took photos in front of it for years and never thought about who created it or what it meant. This time, my daughter asked me what the statue was and what the meaning was. I said, "You know, that's a great question". So, we looked around and we found the title. It is called "Warrior" by none other than Herb Alpert. I instantly got a chill throughout my body. I've grown up listening to Herb Alpert with my father. He taught me about his music. I had only known about him being a sculptor because my dear friend Charlotte was a lifelong fan. I quickly called her and described the statue to her. She confirmed Herb created statue totems. Tears and more tears came. It was a connection with my father who had passed many years ago. I had wished that he could be there with me as I was going through my cancer journey. It turns out on a spiritual level he was there with me all along.

What is even more powerful is that in order to get through treatment and to feel somehow 'normal' while trying to work and still raise my daughter, I focused on what a warrior was, rather than being a worrier. I wanted to find strength to rise up and keep moving. I wore shirts and jewelry with the word WARRIOR on them. Now that I learned that this statue is named "Warrior" I feel even more empowered.

I finally understood my deep connection to this special place. The "Why" suddenly became truly clear. It was a connection with my father. As I passed it during each treatment, my father was there with me in spirit. My daughter and I stood there holding hands and just enjoying the art, energy, and the newly found connection.

I share with all going through cancer journeys, Rise Up Warrior. You are loved. Don't ever underestimate your strength.

We Can-Cer-Vive.

Is there a place or object that helps you feel connected to a loved one?

PART TWO

Gratitude: Where Grace Found Us

Held up in Hope: A Nurse's Prayer and a Promise of Testimony

After receiving the news in the ER about a tumor. I was discharged and walked back to my car. I was in a daze. I am not even sure how I made it to my car. Earlier in the day, I let a nurse friend know I was not feeling well, and we both knew I should go to the ER.

This nurse was a dear friend of mine. Her name is Kenleigh. She rushed to meet me at the parking lot, as she had been checking in with me via text while I was in the ER. We sat in my car and cried.

We just cried.

I don't know how long we were there but together we prayed. I could see in her face and demeanor that my situation was not great. I really needed her to be honest with me because I wanted the truth. Kenleigh guided me along the way over the next few weeks. We had some difficult conversations, but they were important conversations that needed to be had.

My signs and symptoms did not look promising in the beginning. We really had no idea what we were dealing with as there were still so many unknowns. All we knew was that we had to go through the process of testing, appointments, treatments and surgeries.

There was one thing I will always remember during that time we prayed in my car. Kenleigh said that I would get through this and share my testimony with others. At one point, I didn't think that I would have an opportunity to do this. Even if I did make it through this, I didn't know how my words could change things for others.

As I am writing about this event as part of this collection of stories surrounding survival, I am now realizing Kenleigh was right. I am here to share my testimony that we are here to help those around us. To give back. To help lift each other up. Life can take us on many twists and turns, and this is all the more reason to share and support one another.

Sometimes there are no magic words to take away fear or pain. But simply just being present and crying together can bring so much comfort when times are uncertain. I now know this.

Thank you, Kenleigh from the bottom of my heart.

Is there someone in your life who needs a hug? Someone to sit next to and have a good cry? Even sitting together in silence can be extremely powerful.

Tina Calderone-Roth

A Prayer Placed Between Ancient Stones: She Lifted Me Up in Prayer

My close friend Arden is a woman of faith who has supported many in difficult times. There were several occasions where I would find myself saying that she had much more faith in me than I did. Arden was the one who would always find something positive to say, even when things might have been grim.

When I first met her, we started talking about children. She asked me if I had any children and I had to share that at that time I did not. It was a difficult thing to share, but I was not able to have children for 7 years. Arden simply opened her prayer journal and made a notation. "Tina will have a child". To be honest, I thought she was just being nice to make me feel better. The joke was on me, because not too long after, I had my daughter. We would often refer back to that day with such gratitude and joy.

Life went on and I learned from Arden how to try to find the best in others. I have always admired how she was able to build such incredible projects at work that would help to serve so many lives. She has been a true born leader with such powerful vision.

There came a time when work pulled us in different directions, but we always stayed connected. As life handed us challenges, we would often connect to chat and get a renewed sense of perspective. Arden had been dealing with some loss in her family, and she still managed to pull through to help go on a mission trip to Jordan to serve those in need.

The night before she left on her flight, we were able to chat very briefly. It was so hard to ask her for a favor, especially when she was going through so much with the passing of a close loved one. I had something I needed, as I had just received the news of my cancer diagnosis just a couple of days before.

I didn't want gifts; I needed a special prayer. I asked her, as she went on her pilgrimage to the Holy Land after her mission work, to place a prayer in the Western Wall for me. We were both quite emotional given the gravity of the situation. I also let her know that if she was not able to get to the Western Wall, that it was alright because I didn't want to add any pressure to her if she were not able to make it there.

A few days later I received a text from her. She was still away doing her work, so I wondered if she was sending pictures of her journey. As I opened the text, there was this miraculous photo of Arden holding this sign that read: "Healing Prayers for Tina

Roth". Needless to say, there were a significant number of tears streaming down my face. SHE DID IT!!!! Not only that, but she also had other missionary members with her who briefly filmed her walking towards the wall. She placed this prayer for me between the cracks in the ancient stones of the Western Wall. I will be forever humbled by this gesture from the heart.

When I got to meet up with her again after she returned home, we talked and I got the opportunity to thank her. She shared with me that she had just found out a little before the tour left to the Western Wall that her group was already heading to the bus. She was sitting with a little piece of paper, and a pen trying to write in bold letters the prayer for me. Arden almost missed the bus because she was focusing so hard in prayer as she wrote her message. I can't even imagine the pressure she was under with everyone telling her to hurry before she missed the last call.

Arden has the biggest heart and faith beyond what I will ever know. This prayer she left for me, got me through the dark moments after treatment, like day three after chemotherapy. I believe in my heart that this positive energy and prayer lifted me up during my journey. This was indeed the most special gift from a trip overseas.

Thank you, Arden, for your faith and sisterhood.

Has anyone ever lifted you up in prayer or positive thoughts? What are ways we can surround others with positive healing energy?

Lentils for Healing: The Community Came Together with a Food Train

When someone is going through something challenging, it can be difficult to take care of some of the regular day-to-day tasks like grocery shopping, laundry, picking up around the house and cooking. This could not have been truer for my family and me. Between multiple appointments, trying to work, taking our daughter to school, and somewhere finding time to heal, life got rather complex.

Several friends, coworkers, and some from the community all wanted to help in some way. As I work with my clients, I always share that letting people help you when you need it is a good thing. You get help when you need it most, and the folks helping you get the opportunity to serve and support. People genuinely want to help and when we don't get the chance to help, we sometimes feel like we are not doing anything. I have heard this several times over the years.

I must admit, this was not easy for me. I enjoy helping others, but I don't normally feel comfortable accepting help. However, this time was quite different. I was in an entirely different time and world. I truly needed help. My family needed help. This time I accepted help, not just for me, but for the support of my husband and my daughter.

A team at work started a food train that came a couple of times a week and this was an absolute blessing.

My family ate.

This meant so much to me to know that my family were being taken care of. At this time, I could not bend well, and I could not lift or raise my arms. My husband was exhausted running around taking care of all the errands. We were all exhausted. All the more reason the help from the food train provided nourishment and also brought me peace.

My aunt and uncle would come by to drop off the most amazing chicken soup and casseroles. We would save this food and make it stretch for several meals as we were trying to figure out things from one day to the next. These meals were like a hug in a bowl. This was more than just a meal, it was prayer, and a way to show love and care.

One of my dearest friends, Baxter, was there all along the way. Knowing my likes, she prepared homemade lentils in batches. She would bring items over to ensure that I was getting enough protein, as this became a challenge for me. She understood how protein played a crucial role in healing and this made all the difference for me.

Interestingly, along the way, my daughter had a circle of support at school. As I had informed the school that there may be a need to pick up my daughter early due to my planned surgeries, the school looked out for my daughter to ensure she was processing things well. One of her teachers, Ms. Chanda, truly watched over our daughter. She would talk with her. She checked in on her and offered help with her schoolwork if my daughter needed it.

One day, as I was resting after treatment, my daughter came home with a huge bowl of Indian lentils. She shared that her teacher, Ms. Chanda made them because she wanted to help provide nourishment for healing. Let me rephrase this. My daughter's teacher made homemade lentils for the mother of a student. Tears filled my eyes as, I had not ever heard of anything like this before. We were so appreciative of such kindness. Years have gone by and my daughter is now in high school, and she still finds time to stop by to say hi to Ms. Chanda. That sign of gratitude will be a memory we will always carry with us.

I am so grateful for all the care, love and time everyone gave to help our family.

Who in your life might need a bowl of healing soup or a warm comforting casserole perhaps?

It’s More Than Good Manners: The Power of Saying “Thank You”

There are moments in life when the simple act of expressing gratitude can have a profound and lasting impact, both for the person sharing it and as well as the person receiving it. It does not have to be a grand orchestration; it just needs to be from the heart. One such experience stands out vividly in my memory and in my heart.

One day, I found myself waiting outside a coffee shop before a work meeting, having arrived early. As I sat there, I noticed someone in the distance who looked remarkably familiar. After a moment of reflection, I realized it was the surgeon who had operated on me several years prior. Memories of the exceptional care he provided during a crucial surgery quickly returned to me. That procedure was not only significant in itself but also played a pivotal role in helping me uncover a potentially life-threatening diagnosis.

Although I did not want to intrude on his personal time, I felt a strong feeling to speak to him and express my gratitude. I knew it was possible he might not remember me, given the many patients he treats. Nevertheless, I decided to introduce myself. I walked up and greeted him: "Hello, Dr. H, my name is Tina. I am a former patient of yours. I have been doing very well since my surgery, and I want to say thank you so much for the amazing care that you provided me."

I explained that, because of the surgery he performed, I became more attentive to my body, how I was feeling, and my weight. Without that experience, I likely would not have noticed or understood when something was wrong. Two years later, I ended up in the ER, where I discovered my cancer. The unusual weight gain I experienced alerted me to seek help. I would not have known how to pay attention if I had not begun tracking my weight and listening to my body after that surgery two years prior.

I saw his face light up; He shared that he remembered clearly and he was so pleased to see how well I was doing after surgery. Although he was sorry to hear about the cancer diagnosis, he was so pleased to know that I was in tune with my body and noticed that something was wrong.

He gave me the biggest hug and we wished each other well. I will never forget this moment. Although it was a simple chance meeting, the meaning was so powerful. It was meaningful for me, but I also learned that he also was uplifted to hear about how much he is appreciated. I could see how much it meant to him.

The Lasting Value of Gratitude

This chance encounter led me to reflect on the significance of expressing thanks. What does it mean to you when someone thanks you for something? In my observation, these two words are not shared as often as they could or should be. Perhaps we assume that others know we are appreciative. However, taking the time to go back and say those two simple words can truly make a difference.

Who can you go back to and say, "thank you"? Who do you think could benefit from hearing some kind words of gratitude?

Photos for Love and Strength: A Community United for Sarah

During the time of confusion and trying to navigate through complex medical crisis and surgeries in our family, we got the news that our daughter needed to have spinal surgery. As a parent, you will go through great lengths to ensure the safety and wellbeing of your child. Her diagnosis came out of nowhere. Our daughter, Sarah, had been perfectly healthy and fine for all of her life and now having to fathom her going through a spinal surgery just shook us to our core. Tears upon tears and fears upon fears were shared by our little family.

I was not yet well from various surgeries I was going through; I needed to make sure that I was strong enough to be able to support her physically, emotionally and with all my heart. But, having just undergone a surgery a few months before, my strength wasn't quite there. I got the call one day that there was a cancellation for surgery in the early part of June. This would be the perfect timing so Sarah could have the summer to heal and recover.

Sarah had an incredible surgeon. We were grateful beyond belief. We felt safe with him at the helm of this surgery. We were also blessed with an incredible opportunity to have a previous recipient of the same surgery come meet with Sarah and share pieces of advice and support. It was an incredible time to be able to ask questions about normal everyday functioning and to see that there would be light at the end. To this day my daughter and this young lady stay in contact and share milestones.

Logically, we all understood that surgery needed to happen; emotionally, it was another story. I think I was a nervous wreck for the weeks prior to the surgery. My husband had difficulties on the day of surgery, and the night before the surgery Sarah had an extremely difficult time. The gravity of it all hit her like a ton of bricks. We all sat together holding each other crying and praying.

A few days before the surgery I had sent out a request to a couple of friends and family members who could not be here to visit Sarah. I asked that they wear something green that represents scoliosis awareness and to take a quick snapshot of themselves with a message showing encouragement. It was meant to go out to maybe 5 people at most. What ended up happening was word spread and the entire hospital room, walls and window were covered with pictures and words of encouragement and support for her. Friends from school, family, teachers, neighbors, and people from out of state were all sending over photos to encourage her and lift her up. Everybody commented when they walked into the room because it was in fact scoliosis awareness month in June. It was this simple act of kindness that brought so much joy, light and love to a young girl who really needed it during such a frightening time. It was awe inspiring to stand there amongst all the encouragement and love. Sarah was truly surrounded by love and light.

I can still recall the first night after surgery: we were all nervous, exhausted and anxious as to the next steps. Without much sleep in the hospital, the next morning came. The sun poured through the blinds. It was at that moment that I realized we made it through the storm. We made it to the next day. Sarah made it through the night and was about to embark on her journey of healing. She was resilient then and continues to be to this day.

When the hard times came over the following weeks, she would look at all the photos and signs that were posted in her room. We will always treasure these expressions of love and encouragement. It was from a simple form of asking a couple of people for help that turned into a movement for support and lifting up a child in need.

I believe that we often fall into this thought process that something simple may not carry much value or meaning. I am here to share that a simple act of kindness can change a life. If it is from the heart with positive intent, you can't go wrong.

What are some ways that you can offer support to someone you know? What about someone in the community? What about a neighbor, shelter, or the local community center?

When the Diagnosis Was on Mute: The Night Music Carried Me

Music, Friendship, and The Power of a Live Performance

Music, art, and live performances have always been a meaningful part of my life. Many of my closest friends share these passions, and attending concerts has been a lifelong tradition for us. There is something special about the energy exchanged between the artists and the audience. It is a feeling that always left me invigorated and inspired. When my friend Charlotte mentioned an upcoming festival, featuring many of the bands we loved in high school and college, she went ahead and purchased tickets for us. Unfortunately, the pandemic put those plans on hold for a year.

Facing Uncertainty and a Difficult Diagnosis

Eventually, the concert was rescheduled, and Charlotte was excited for us to attend and enjoy the music together. However, I had recently spent time in the ER, where I received troubling news about my health. Charlotte believed that attending the concert would bring me some much-needed joy during such an uncertain time, but I was not in a good place physically or emotionally. Despite my love for music, I was unwell and declined her invitation several times. With test results still pending and a surgery scheduled for the following week, I found myself in a dark place. I could not fathom going to an all-day concert at a time like this.

Support and Encouragement

I expressed my gratitude to Charlotte for the gift of the tickets and suggested she find someone else to go with her, as I did not feel that I would be able to attend. One day, she came to my home and, without any pressure, shared with me that she truly believed I needed to go to this concert. She knew how much joy it would bring. In that moment, we both realized, without a word spoken, that, given the uncertainty of my health, this could be the last concert I would attend. I agreed to try my best to make it, and Charlotte kindly reassured me that we could leave early or return home if necessary.

The Day of the Concert Festival

On the day of the event, I still wasn't feeling well. I dressed comfortably in tennis shoes and casual clothes, shielding myself from the sun and heat. I took things slowly, stopping as needed to rest and hydrate throughout the all-day event. Despite my fatigue, I found myself enjoying the experience and just taking things slowly.

A Moment of Joy

When Bauhaus, the band we were most excited to see, came on stage, they performed all their hits with incredible energy. For that hour, I was cheering, singing, and dancing, on my feet. The joy I felt wiped away my fear and anguish. The music drowned out my pain and worries about the future. For that brief moment, I experienced a respite from the heaviness of my situation. It was like my diagnosis was on mute for that time being.

The Diagnosis

A week and a half after the concert, I learned that I had cancer. I knew that the road ahead would be rough, but the joy I experienced at the concert was something I was able to carry with me and reflect on during the next several months. I would play the music on my phone and reflect on the great memories created that day.

I don't know how my friend Charlotte knew how important this would be for me and us. She made it happen. She had this magic of making it happen and it all brought me so much joy and peace.

Thank you, Charlotte as we were "searching for Satori". I believe we found it.

Has there been an event that has helped you through a challenging time? Has there ever been a person who helped encourage you to see things from a different perspective? Did you give them a chance?

Oh, The Places Cancer Took Me

Having gone through the diagnosis and all the phases of it, it's taking me to many different places on the map. I initially wanted to go on with what I thought would be our last family vacation. So, despite not feeling well and having pain or discomfort, we were on a plane to Niagara Falls.

That was my goal. I wanted to see the falls before my end days.

We went as a family, and we experienced the beautiful energy of Niagara Falls. We had an incredible time; there's something very magical about that place. I hope to return someday.

After that, we jumped on a flight over to Boston, because I wanted to show my daughter the Freedom Trail and to be able to toss tea into the harbor. Seeing her do that just brought me so much joy. She got to operate an amphibious duck boat in the Charles River and it's something I'm going to remember for the rest of my life.

We flew to Colorado for my commencement ceremony, took a day trip over to Breckenridge and had an incredible time. We got to see the Troll sculpture and learned about the area. We also got to see the Continental Divide.

Part of my journey has taken me to different parts of California such as Imperial Beach. Here, I got to meet the most incredible tattoo artist who brought me so much confidence and support. I am forever grateful. In Tennessee, I got to get connected again with my family and to be able to stand on the stage of the Grand Old Opry and sing "You Are My Sunshine". We spent time in Santa Barbara sitting on the wharf and enjoy the cool, tranquil breeze. In the making of this book, I got the pleasure of connecting with an editor in England and artists in Nigeria. How incredible that my little stories would end up being worked on internationally. I never could have imagined this.

I've learned that one never truly knows where our path will lead us, but I do know this. We have to be or learn to be receptive to what is going on around us. It could be something as difficult as removing toxicity from your life; celebrating small wins; letting your family and friends know how much you love them and how much they mean to you or letting others know how much you appreciate them.

We are all in this world together.

I can't help to think and reflect upon how I would not be here today without all the lives that have come into my life to support me and encourage me during the darkest times. Someone very special, Vance, once told me that we need to "stop living in fear and live in love". When I first heard this, I wasn't quite sure what that really meant. I just thought OK, don't be fearful. But as I reflected deeper upon the decisions I made in my life, I realized I was living my life out of fear. I think this is in part due to my profession and how I was raised.

In the field of social work and care management you tend to create a contingency plan for your cases, almost as if you have to have a back up to the backup plan because things will go awry for various reasons. I incorporated this mentality into my life. Having a contingency plan because something is likely going to fall apart. Almost setting yourself up for a self-fulfilling prophecy. So now I'm learning to go along for the ride and to just know that there will be twists and turns and some bumps along the way.

I'm thinking about all those who have come into my life, physical therapists, nurses, x-ray technicians, medical providers, surgeons, specialists, therapists, tattoo artists, makeup artists, manicurists, and massage therapists, and I realize I would not be here today without the care, service and attention being bestowed upon me.

Life is short and I want to celebrate every moment of it. I had to learn how to move on from toxic situations and to value myself and to advocate for my family. Now, I know I have to pay it forward to those who may be in similar situations that I went through. Writing this book has been something so special to me, being able to capture these events that were happening in my life every day was so important to me. At first glance they may appear to be very simple on the surface, but they were much deeper on a whole different level. There's so much going on in our world today that I thought it was important to share something positive that is happening all around us.

Have you had to deal with a diagnosis or situation that led you to different people and places that you would not have normally been connected with? How has this enriched who you are?

Capturing a Moment: The Meaning of The Commencement Speech

It was during the surge of the global pandemic that I decided that I needed to go back to school. The goal was to learn how I could continue to contribute and promote wellness in my community. I signed up and met with my guidance counselor & decided that I would earn my 2nd master's degree in healthcare administration through an online program. This school was located in another state. Then all of a sudden, I was informed that I was accepted and that I had just made the cut off to start in two weeks' time. I thought to myself, oh my gosh, what have I done?

It was not easy working full-time managing multiple medical clinics during the most intense time in the history of healthcare. But if I had to do it all over again, I would gladly do so without hesitation.

I had the opportunity to learn from some of the most incredible professors who have the most impressive credentials. Being able to learn from my classmates from different states and countries was such a fantastic opportunity. Topics of government, history, equality, social determinants of health, ethics, death, dignity, community, and empowerment were present in each of my courses.

I decided to go back to school, as I shared earlier to better myself so that I could serve my community. I also went back to set an example for my amazing daughter, Sarah, who was there with me along the way. She was there writing me notes to encourage me and cheered me on when I completed my assignments. We would sit together and do homework.

Midway through my program, I did not feel well. I landed in the hospital and was diagnosed with ovarian cancer. My world as I knew it was over. I, who had worked in healthcare for over 25 years, became a patient. I was vulnerable and lost. There were so many unknowns, fear, confusion, and not knowing what was to be. The one thing I did know was that I was not going to give up my schooling. Even in the hospital and during chemo, I would take my laptop to keep up with my assignments. I did this because now more than ever, I understood the importance of making changes in healthcare. I saw the gaps and I started advocating.

I was surrounded by much love and support from so many and I am forever grateful. Friends, family, support groups, my work families, women around the world who are Sisters in Teal Power, and my community. The challenging part was, I needed to have surgery pretty quickly, but I was also in the last leg of my master's program. I didn't want to give it up. I reached out to my professor and asked if I could turn in my capstone project early. This was an odd request: who would ask to turn in a capstone project early?

I explained that I had to have surgery and I shared a brief summary of what I was experiencing.

My professor, who was known to be a "by the book" teacher and had very high expectations for his classes, suddenly paused and offered support. He was based in several states away and asked if he and his family could pray for me. I was so overwhelmed with appreciation. In my heart, one's faith is important. If someone has a different faith than mine and they offer me a prayer or blessing, this is beautiful gift. I was and still am so honored.

My family laughs at me, because there is a photo of me in the hospital after surgery and I am in the hospital bed with my laptop on a table so that I could get my weekly assignment turned in. I actually worked harder so that I could get things done early. Once everything was done and I hit the submit button for my final course, I found that I passed and I would be able to graduate.

I had no plans of going to the commencement ceremony, because I had already done this many years ago for my first masters. However, something changed. My professor sent me the most incredible message. He shared that he hoped I would be able to attend the ceremony so that he could personally shake my hand.

After much planning, we made it there. With my family in the massive stadium, we were there. To make matters even more special, I was selected to give the commencement speech. I was so nervous. I stood there behind the podium and did everything I could to keep it together. All the while, my professor was sitting behind me. At the end I got to meet him in person and give him, not a handshake, a hug. This man opened my eyes to see beyond the limited scope that I was viewing healthcare from. He encouraged me during the darkest time in my life. It is this human connection that makes all the difference.

I have learned that we are a community, we flourish when we share our gifts, talents, and passions. I am thankful for this impactful time that helped me to advocate for those who may not feel able to speak for themselves when they are not feeling well or are near the end of life.

I am humbled and forever grateful for my degree and I am so inspired on ways that I can use my gained knowledge to drive change and support the underserved in healthcare.

Who has supported you during challenging times? Has someone you did not consider ever come forward to offer support? Who can you offer support to?

PART THREE

Healing: Learning to be Whole

Wrapped in Grace: Finding Peace Through the Anointing of the Sick

I had been dealing with a cancer diagnosis that came out of nowhere. We were all blindsided to say the least. In my first year of treatment and surgery, I had well over 168 appointments for everything and anything. Your life becomes a schedule. Appointments included chemotherapy, hydration infusions, physical therapy, counseling, lab work, an array of testing, port flushes, specialist appointments and so on. I think at some point I was not really able to fully grasp the gravity of what was happening because I was basically just going through the motions. The most important thing for me was trying to keep it together for my daughter, who was just ten years old at the time.

One thing I can remember was wanting to ask the cancer center social worker Yoshi for help. Yoshi knew my faith and she understood how one's faith is part of the healing process. I wanted to know if I could receive the Anointing of the Sick sacrament, but I was nervous about asking. Yoshi was a very special person with so much positive energy. She had a gift of knowing what to say at the exact right moment. This became even more evident during one of my rounds of treatment. As they say, God works in mysterious ways, and I could not agree more. As I was contemplating how to ask for her guidance on this, she, with the biggest heart, wanted to ask if she could help me with the anointing...at the same time. She graciously arranged for me to receive the sacrament at one of my treatments.

I was full of many emotions. Many thoughts and questions came flooding through my head. Did this mean that I was giving up? Was I going to die? How would life be after? What would happen next? I am unable to express what a beautiful moment it was to receive the anointing and blessing. Heavy sobbing and tears were shed that day. The priest was so kind and so full of light and grace, that I felt at peace.

Later that night I fell into a deep sleep, which is a miracle in and of itself with all the nausea after treatment. When I awoke the next morning, I felt like a new person. I felt that whatever came my way, I was going to handle it well and move forward. I no longer had the fear of the unknown. I was at peace. Something happened to me; I was no longer carrying a heavy load of fear. I knew in my heart that all I could do was to live my life day by day and to the fullest. I put everything into God's hands, as it was no longer my burden to carry. This was much bigger than me.

I'm in love with life. I now live to enjoy time with those I love. I am determined to serve my community and to give back. I am committed to supporting others who are going through similar journeys. I have learned that we are all connected and that we all have gifts to share with others.

I received so much from my anointing. I received LIFE.

Have you or someone you know ever received a special blessing, or prayer? If so, how did it feel after? Was there comfort or peace?

The Little Blue Cap

Sometimes the simplest of things can evoke much emotion and create lasting memories. Never did I think this would happen with an insignificant object that is normally discarded at the time of use. I also was not aware of how a little blue cap would show me how fragile life is.

It has been over three years since I underwent surgery and chemotherapy as part of my cancer treatment plan. It was a time that I still don't think I have fully processed, even to this day. All I know is that I am in love with life and hope to create many lasting memories with those who have been with me on this journey.

As you go through surgery and chemotherapy, the experience is quite different for each person. In speaking of my own personal journey, there was so much going on all at once.

Appointments, labs, treatment and recovery were all things to navigate. It was challenging to fully grasp that I actually made it through. Things seem to come at you at warp speed. Someone once shared with me that each round of chemo is its own journey. When I first heard this, I was confused. To me round two would be like one and so on. But little did I know how wrong I was.

As I was working and trying to finish up my second master's degree, I was going through chemo treatments; it may not have been my smartest move to not take a leave of absence, but I really needed to do this to keep my mind and spirit focused on something bigger than me. I immediately learned that I was not made of steel, and I quickly was challenged with how I needed to ask for help. This was something I never wanted to do. I was proud to be independent and an incredible multitasker. Now, I was faced with needing help with the most mundane things like carrying my purse and pouring a cup of tea. Needless to say, it was a blow to my spirit.

About two weeks into my first round of chemo, IV hydration was required. With all the IVs going on, one learns quite a lot about ports, IVs, flushing ports, and hydration. It just becomes common place.

This went on for months.

I got really good at administering my own hydration via my port. I had incredible nurses who taught me very well. My home became a mini clinic with all the durable medical equipment, supplies and medications.

I would hydrate for two to three days after treatment. Bags of normal saline, and heparin flushes were organized and in place at my home. Once a bag is set up on an IV pole, you have to remove the little blue cap to help gravity do its thing. This was something I did all the time: it was nothing out of the ordinary. After each hydration was completed, everything was quickly disposed of and life went on.

As time passed, I completed all my rounds of chemo. Slowly, I focused on trying to regain my strength and endurance. I was moving forward months later, and my heart was so thrilled to feel 'normal' again...whatever that meant. One day, I was outside watering plants and off to the corner of my eye I saw something on the front patio. It was a little blue thing. As my eyes focused, I immediately knew what it was. It was a little blue cap from a hydration bag. I have no idea how it got there, or how no one had seen it before.

As I stood there staring at this insignificant little thing, tears instantly were running down my face. I realized at that moment that I had made it through the surgeries and treatments. I had a love-hate relationship with this little blue cap. On the one hand it represented the most painful and darkest feelings I have ever known. However, on the other hand, it also was part of something that helped save my life. I stood there sobbing. My husband rushed out because he thought I had fallen. When I showed him the little blue cap, he went to throw it away to help me not to be sad.

I asked him not to throw it away; I sat down and held it in my hands, and a wave of memories and emotions came rushing over me. We hugged each other with tears in our eyes, tears of joy that I had life and we had so much to be thankful for. The little blue cap represented the fears that I had, and I decided that I did not want fear and pain to live on. I wanted to turn something so difficult into something positive and to embrace it. This became extremely important to me. I then took the little blue cap and incorporated it into a 3D painting of a butterfly soaring high up into the sky. To this day, I reflect on that painting as a symbol of how meaning and life can come out of something so unimportant and how there is so much to be grateful for.

Even if it is just a little blue cap.

What challenging item/memory can you turn into something positive/empowering?

My Oncologist: The Doctor Who Healed My Spirit

Reflections Three Years Later

It has now been three years since I first met with my oncologist. It was a period marked by multiple surgeries, and treatments. Even now, I find it difficult to believe that I am on this side of the cancer journey. Throughout this experience, I have been fortunate to receive exceptional care and unwavering support, for which I am eternally grateful.

The Impact of Diagnosis

Receiving the diagnosis was a life-altering moment that shook me to my core. No one wants to hear the words "It is Cancer". The journey began with the realization that something was wrong, followed by countless tests, the confirmation of the diagnosis, and treatment. Life quickly transformed into a vast sea of appointments. The most challenging part of it all was that it did not impact just me. It weighed heavily on my family and support system.

Living Through Treatment

During my first year alone, I attended over 168 appointments. These included port flushes, chemotherapy sessions, bloodwork, genetic testing, scans, surgeries, medical check-ups, physical therapy, counseling, group sessions, family counseling, imaging, hydration, infusions, and more. Eventually, everything became routine, and I grew numb to the process, as my entire existence revolved around appointments. Life was strictly regimented, and I found myself unable to see beyond the next scheduled visit. I clung desperately to anything that made me feel "normal," whatever that meant for me at the time.

The One Constant

With the world spinning around my family and myself, there was one constant. My Oncologist, Dr. Sharma; when I first found out that I needed to be referred to oncology, I knew that I wanted Dr. Sharma to be my doctor. I had known him in work life. However, the situation changed, I was now a patient. I have to repeat this again: I was now a patient. This left pain in my heart. I did not know how to be a patient. In the field of social work, I aimed to take care of others for years. I was out of my element as a patient.

Dr. Sharma, from day one, talked with me. We would actually talk. I was not just a patient; I was a person. He saw me as a person. He advocated for me and guided me through the next steps. I still remember one thing he said to me on my very first appointment. He shared, “You will do well with treatment and surgery, because you have a positive outlook”. At first, I was not really sure what to make of this. However, as time moved on, his words were true. I found that going through the journey with an open mind and heart was the best way for me to approach this for my family.

At every appointment, Dr. Sharma treated me and listened to me. He heard my fears. He guided me and brought me comfort. On some days we would laugh and other times we would sit and talk about possible challenges. There was a respect and the exam room really was a safe place for me, when previously I was reluctant due to not wanting to hear bad news.

Life After Treatment

When the appointments finally began to end, and the treatments concluded, I was left wondering what would come next. During one of my last appointments with Dr. Sharma, I was informed that future visits would be annually and tests would become less frequent. This is what we all wanted, but I was nervous, because I was in a place that I did not quite understand. What this meant was, I was now on the other side of cancer and treatment. I really did not know what to do with myself or what I needed to do next. Dr. Sharma told me that this milestone was something to celebrate and that I had completed treatment and was now "FREE."

I questioned what "free" truly meant. I asked what I was supposed to do now. I was so confused because now, I could resume more of a normal life. Dr. Sharma's response was simple: "Live your life and to continue to do good work in the community." I found myself lost, unsure how to move forward without the familiar structure that had defined my days during this cancer journey. Yet, through it all, I came to realize that I was still here. I was still standing. This may sound crazy, but this was a really hard time.

As I moved forward, I kept Dr. Sharma's words in my heart. I knew that I had to give back. I was so blessed to receive all that I had. I know that we are all connected and I need to give to others faced with similar challenges. I moved on to a new job serving those in need, we resumed volunteering every weekend, we donated, we advocated and to this day my family I try to support our community however we can.

After the Bell Was Rung.

On my final day of chemotherapy, we all gathered outside the cancer center donned in teal to represent my cancer and we RANG a bell given to me by a special person Jamie. I rang that bell with all that I had. It was a victorious time for us all, including Dr. Sharma. He came to this ringing event and celebrated with us. This was as much of a victory for him as it was for me. He got me to the other side.

In the end, all I know is that I have been given a second chance of life. I am blessed. My daughter, who was ten at the time of my diagnosis, has me here and that is the best feeling. I do not know what the future has in store for me, but in my heart, I know I have to stay positive, work on removing negativity in my life and to serve others in need. I aim to live up to the words that Dr.

Sharma gave me. He not only treated my diagnosis, he treated my spirit.

Thank you, Dr. Sharma, for the incredible care you gave me and for giving me life.

Who has guided you through a challenging time? Do they know how much you appreciate them? How can you express your gratitude?

The Courage to Heal: My Therapy Was a Badge of Honor

As I was going through the early phases of treatment, next steps with surgery, and trying to support my family for a period, I didn't really know where to begin. I suddenly felt overwhelmed. I knew I had to move forward, but I wasn't quite sure how. I quickly learned that I needed to initiate therapy for myself to help process and to help support my family with this cancer diagnosis.

Being that in person therapy was going to be challenging for me physically, I went online and found a therapist. I was not certain what to look for, as I was not even clear on how to describe what I was going through. In my life as a care manager in the field of social work, I would support others in locating a therapist for themselves; I would pose questions to get my clients to think about the following: in person or virtual therapy, the gender of the provider, the type of treatment need, and to level set that the first provider selected may not end up being the right fit. I would share that it has to be the right fit and to be open and willing to do the work. Therapy is not easy, but it is in the hard work and commitment that we learn, heal and grow.

I selected a provider for myself. I did not know if it was going to be a right fit or not, but I knew I had to get started somewhere. Availability was probably a key factor, so I selected this one gentleman, who we will call David. He covered my area where I lived and he had availability. In his profile I noted that he had a strong military background. For some reason, I felt this would be helpful in establishing boundaries and clarity. I cannot explain how or why, I just had feeling. I did not know how I would feel speaking to a male provider given there was a lot of very personal things that I thought I might feel more comfortable discussing if I had a female provider. But again, I realized I had to get started and give it a try.

After my very first session with David, I knew it was going to be very impactful. He gave me so much to think about and encouraged me to look at things from a different angle. David encouraged me to think about root causes. He helped me to look at my language and my view of myself. These were things that I really never thought about before. I learned that I was not extending grace to myself and was quite hard on myself.

He referred to me as resilient with going through all of this therapy, chemotherapy, treatment, surgeries, and while working and going to school. We would laugh about it, and I laughed because I never thought of myself as tough. Here he was with years of military experience, and we were talking about me being strong and full of grit. I still chuckle about it every now and again. I am more of a craft/artsy person, and I really didn't see myself with much strength. David taught me to extend grace to myself. With his guidance, I learned not to downplay what was going on because it was in fact, life changing. There were many sessions where I just cried because things were frightening. There was a lot of unknown...and it was ongoing. There were some sessions where I would share that not having answers, not knowing if I was going to live or not was so overwhelming.

David was there for almost 3 years to help me through this process. We went through many different phases of my cancer journey. When I first started therapy with David, I had hair and then one day I didn't. David got me through the darkest time in my life. I've always felt that we have to respect cancer because cancer knows what it's doing. I didn't realize that I was full of fear. That I was living my life in fear. I didn't know if I was going to live or not. In addition, the whole issue with scanxiety is very real and this is something that we worked on for quite some time. When going through something like cancer, you take multiple tests, scans, and bloodwork. Each time, I would see that my lab results would be ready via the application on my phone, and I would freeze. I wanted to see the results, but I didn't want to look. This went on for at least the first two years.

I can't recommend enough how important it is for us to take part in therapy. It could be challenging in the beginning, but it is something that helps open our minds to something much bigger. I learned that I had to get out of the situation I was in to move on and to not live in fear and with guilt. We can't let people control us. I look back now on the past three, almost four years, and I have a smile on my face because I've grown. I am not the same person I was before. I am stronger and I think David and I are both in agreement that a cancer diagnosis is not what anybody wants. However, my diagnosis helped me find my voice, and for this, I am grateful.

Thank you, David, for the peace you have given me.

Can therapy be a support? Are you open to learning more about yourself and how you can grow, or heal perhaps?

Beautifully Broken: You Don't Have to Carry It Alone

After attending several support groups and therapy sessions, I found that focusing on mantras or phrases can help capture feelings and emotions. The following were recurring phrases, mantras and feelings that would seem to come up time and time again when I was going through treatment. I would often sit and reflect on these phrases. I tried to capture as many as I could. Now, in retrospect, I could not be prouder to be broken and made new.

As the saying goes, when you love someone, you will go through great lengths. My child is my reason for being and she gave me strength to keep moving forward. I shared these thoughts and words with her because I wanted her to see that there would be challenges in life. That it is OK to feel lost, because it is in that searching for oneself that we truly grow.

What I learned so far is that life can be messy, but it is in that messiness that lends itself to such incredible beauty, talents, gifts, meaning and connection. I often reflect on the art of Kintsugi, the Japanese art of repairing broken pottery with precious metals and stones. In the end the pottery becomes even more stunning as it transforms into a priceless piece of art. We are in essence beautifully broken. This originally made me sad, but now looking back, I am proud and renewed. I am grateful for the work done in my sessions and groups.

Here are the phrases that were present in my life, as they would often flow by and circle round again. I tried to categorize them with certain themes here.

I am (a):

Warrior, friend, bad ass, renegade, fashionista, mentor, graduate, mother, wife, advocate, volunteer, patient, leader, follower, recipient, confident, standing tall, scarred, vulnerable, adjuster, pivoter, problem solver, believer, sharer, faithful, supporter, advocate, a woman of faith...

I feel:

Faith over fear, I-can-cer-vive, tired, pain, weak, strong, numb, loved, secure, tranquil, renewed, creative, colorful, anchored in hope, purposeful, healed, supported, dedicated, blessed, adventurous, NED, lost, found, positive, changes...

I have:

Sisterhood of friends, mutation, teal sisters, power, fun, reflection, a learning to live, questions, gratitude, a new beginning, started over, ended a chapter, started a new chapter, smiles, husband, tears, faith, grief, trust, grace, been tested, LIFE, been anointed, a child, been blessed, light, friendship, fog, trust, reflection, sacred spaces, experience, a journey, perspective, Grit, Teal Power, positive mindset, growth, empowerment, searched, purple love, soul, to face it and move on, stories to tell…

I need:

A higher power, a lifeline, retreat, nature walks, trees, storytelling, dancing, meditation sound bath, yoga, to write, know my limits, a vision board, to fight like a girl, manifestation, to give back, communication, connection, live for the moments, balance, grace, a new story, light, to just keep going, smile, stay positive, hugs, laughter, trust, art, music, purpose, faith, sharing, validation, support, reconnection, to search for satori (enlightenment), the " why", prayer, renewal, long drives, to try, silence, reflection, to grow, time in a bottle, support, to live, to fight for me…

I want to give:

Storytelling, love, peace, comfort, empowerment, inspiration, connection, trust, grace, spreading of love, light, validation, support, relatability, prayer, connection…

These words were captured because I learned from support groups I was in about how to capture feelings, journaling and sharing.

The Power of Support Groups:

Being in the field of social work and care management for over 25 years, I have encouraged many clients and families to connect with various support groups. I never imagined how much they would have an impact on my life. Trying to move forward with a not great diagnosis of cancer, I quickly learned that I needed to reach out and connect with others going through a similar journey.

At my first support group meeting, I was surprised to find a room full of people who genuinely listened and cared. Some were at the beginning of their journey. Some were actively in treatment, and others had years of experience. As everyone spoke their truths, I quickly realized they shared not just similar symptoms but also similar emotions, fears, and hopes.

The group offered a safe space to talk openly, exchange practical tips, and offer emotional encouragement. We have loved ones around to help us, but there is something about sharing with someone who has walked in your shoes that can make all the difference.

I was not alone in my fears.

The stories that were graciously shared with me gave me hope and practical tools to manage my day-to-day life. I will forever hold the stories shared with me in my heart.

I found answers to the things that were happening to me. Our medical providers treat us clinically, but there is the real day to day that also needs to be addressed. I found answers to questions that truly helped me function when I wasn't sure I could.

During a cancer retreat by Healing Odessey, we were located up the mountains, I drove up the hills not knowing what do make of the next couple of days. When I came down the hills to return home, I was full of life. I learned a lot about myself. We encouraged and supported each other. The immense support for one another while we climbed a high telephone pole and zipped lined, still gives me chills. It was such an incredible experience that I will always carry with me. Several of us were unsteady on our feet when we first arrived. I was dealing with general weaknesses and pain, but we all did what we could and were stronger for it.

I was connected with another group called Cancer Kinship; We had the most heartfelt sessions of sharing. We painted, had tea, we learned so much about how to care for ourselves. The validation received help us lift some of the heavy weight of fear that we all carried, especially when trying to deal with the diagnosis, treatment and managing to live a 'normal' life.

My daughter was surrounded by care and light with an incredible program called Camp Kesem, which is truly magic. A child dealing with a parent who has cancer is difficult and my daughter received so much joy and a chance to just be a kid for a while.

A closing thought:

This roller coaster ride with cancer is something that is lifelong: it doesn't end after treatment. Living a life where you have to deal with scanxiety is not for the faint of heart. Working through fear, anxiety, stress, pain, and the unknown are all areas that one needs to navigate on an ongoing basis.

To keep empowered, it is vital that survivors of cancer and other life-altering events stay connected with others. Support groups have been a lifeline for myself and my family. Let's face it, a disease like cancer impacts our entire society. Impowering each other and lifting each other up during crisis is healing for us all. Through my time with support groups such as Cancer Kinship, and others online, I found strength, hope, and the courage to keep moving forward. Members support each other through setbacks and celebrate even the smallest victories. I made lasting relationships that have greatly enriched my life. We need to remember when facing challenges and feeling alone, that there are people ready to stand with you. The hardest and bravest step is reaching out for support.

What are some powerful mantras that have meaning for you? How can you interweave them into your daily life? How can they guide you with deeper connection?

Are there any support groups or programs who have helped support you or your loved ones? How can we share the importance of what support groups can do for others going through challenging times?

How can we offer support to support groups?

Becoming Visible Once Again: Reclaiming the Mirror

Getting our hair and nails done, putting on make-up and even getting a tattoo are things that are part of our everyday culture.

Professional hair stylists, make-up artists, nail technicians and tattoo artists help individuals to highlight their unique style and to also help have positive feelings of self. Whether experimenting with bold makeup looks, intricate nail art, the latest hairstyles, or meaningful tattoos, each choice can reflect personal tastes and identity. I always had an appreciation for these professionals, but never did I think how much I would hold them in my heart, as I have in the past three years.

When I went through surgery and chemotherapy, I changed. I evolved into a deeper level of self. I know it sounds crazy, but something happened. I no longer was the same person I once was. I previously thought of myself as helpful, and now I still aim to be helpful, but now I aim to serve and to support truly from my heart. However, with that being said, I may have found myself, but I physically changed...and I changed dramatically.

When you start chemotherapy different things happen. One such area is side effects. All sorts of things can happen, and they can vary quite drastically from one person to the next. One common thing is hair loss and for some reason day 13 and 14 are the days I noticed hair loss. I knew this was coming and I figured I wanted to live, and losing my hair was not important. However, I did not realize how powerful that experience would be. It was not just me it affected. My family, my work, and those around me had to deal with the adjustment. I was perceived differently and there's this sense of loss and a longing to feel "normal" whatever that really means. I went through different head caps, wigs, lashes painted on eyebrows. You name it, I bought it and I went through it all.

You feel like a fraction of yourself. I did believe in being true to myself, however it was challenging to try and find ways to adjust. When you're going through treatment and you're going through different changes, you physically morph in phases. I would say roughly about every three months I was changing and I had to adjust. When your hair does start to grow back it comes out in weird ways and your hair texture changes. The growth rate is different on different parts of your head and it's a whole adjustment process. I went through several hairdos. I bleached my hair. I cut it. I changed the colors. I wouldn't have been able to adjust without the love, grace and support of the most amazing hair stylists.

❀ Tina Calderone-Roth

From the bottom of my heart, I thank all the beauticians that helped support me, encouraged me and lifted me up. They went through all of this together with me and I am forever grateful.

I didn't know how to wear makeup anymore because my skin changed. The texture changed and everything was different. The same makeup that I had worn for years before wouldn't work anymore. I went to see these amazing makeup artists who really helped me, and I found a fresh style, and a new me. I was bolder and it was so exciting. Instead of being sad they helped bring me joy and self-confidence. I started wearing a bold red lipstick and gorgeous lashes. I had a new look, and it was fun.

I would need help with pedicures and manicures during treatment. I developed some neuropathy and so cutting nails and things like that were really challenging for me. I felt weak. I just hurt everywhere. When I went to have a pedicure or manicure the technicians there were so incredible. We would share stories and they supported me with aromatherapy, and it made so much of a difference...and I felt special. Very special.

I had surgery and I was left with many scars that I didn't know how to address. I was referred to a tattoo artist for help. I never had a tattoo and that was in part because I could never really commit to a design. I was apprehensive and upset about having to get a tattoo to help address something challenging not something by choice. I was very conflicted by this. I met the most incredible tattoo artist who was recommended by a very dear friend, and I am forever grateful. This tattoo artist handled my situation with such grace, dignity and compassion. We talked, we exchanged stories from the heart and there was true connection and meaning. After undergoing the tattoo art that she did for me, and I say art because it is truly an art form. I feel whole again. I am whole now. Thank you, Laura.

I am sharing these brief accounts because I believe that many hairstylists, artisans, and technicians may not fully appreciate the significant role they play in supporting individuals experiencing major physical changes. I now feel whole again because of the wonderful care and attention that I received from these specialists. From my heart to yours, I thank you.

What gifts/talents do you have that you can help others with? You never know, you could change a life. What stylist, technician, artist, can you thank?

The Runway of Resilience: Scarred, Styled and Standing Strong

When I attend a cancer survivor model fashion show, I am awe struck by the courage and beauty radiating from the runway. Watching each survivor model share their story of diagnosis, treatment, and resilience is so empowering. As they come forward to celebrate life, I am moved by the sense of hope and solidarity that is beaming outward from each model. The room is always filled with such joy, love and light.

These events don't just highlight stylish outfits; they show the powerful journeys of each person who has faced cancer head-on. Their presence encourages everyone to embrace early detection, challenge misconceptions, and recognize the strength that lies within.

For me, these fashion shows also feel deeply meaningful as fundraisers. The energy and generosity from those who attend helps fuel research, advance patient care, and strengthen advocacy programs that touch countless lives—including my own family. The combination of heartfelt stories, community support, and shared purpose transforms what could be a typical event into a beacon of compassion and change. In these moments, it's clear that together, we make a real difference in the fight against cancer.

At the first fashion show I attended, I was honored to receive an invite by Yoli, the founder of Cancer Kinship, to give the opening invocation/prayer to start off the event. On that evening Yoli later asked me to join her as a model in the fashion show the following year. To be honest with you, I thought there would be no way I could do this. I was not a model. I didn't see myself walking a catwalk. I was dealing with generalized weakness, and I, in the middle of multiple surgeries, was having challenges with walking, tripping and falling. I had scars on top of scars. I did not feel that I would be a good representation of a cancer model.

As time passed, I got to know Yoli and her amazing heart and passion to support those battling cancer. She had this gift of helping others feel at peace and like family. I attended several events that she and her nonprofit program hosted. There was a series of events that she put together. They were a summer series of empowerment sessions. Together we learned about self-care after going through cancer treatments. There was this instant sisterhood...a fellowship. We were in a safe space. We learned about make up, we did art therapy, and we shared. At the end of the summer, the group would join in a fashion show to help raise not only money, but awareness for additional support services for those in need.

The fashion show was called the "Brave, Bold and Boundless" Fashion Show by Caner Kinship. We would each walk the catwalk in three different outfits. Because I was dealing with the loss of my hair, I had been struggling with what feeling feminine would mean for me. I wanted to feel strong and beautiful all at once. As I reflected on what beautiful and strong would look like, an idea came to me. The color that represents ovarian cancer is teal. With this in mind, I went online and found teal colored boxing gloves. I have to share, I am not aware of all things boxing, but I really had an appreciation for the idea of fighting to live. I wanted to represent tough and being glamourous at the same time. I then took the boxing gloves and blinged them out with all kinds of crystal stones.

I wore these gloves with an evening gown as I walked the catwalk. I was so afraid of tripping or falling, but something magical happened. I felt as if I was floating. Being surrounded by so much love and support lifted me up. Here I was trying to do something good for others, and yet I was the one being loved on. It was a truly emotional moment to see loved ones and strangers cheer for you. These blinged out boxing gloves have become a treasure and symbol of resilience for me.

After this event, I had so many new close friends who together were on this meandering journey of healing. I learned about adjusting to change. I started wearing fun clothes, big sunglasses, and new makeup. I was learning about my new self. I was learning to live again.

None of this would have been possible without the heart that Yoli has shared with so many. I don't know how she does it, but she is truly a ray of light, hope and love.

Have you ever met an inspiring person in your community? What causes are close to your heart? How can we pass this inspiration on to others?

PART FOUR

Legacy: What Remains is Human Connection

Summary Reflection

I personally want to thank you for reading along with this collection of stories with me. Initially, I was uncertain if I could do this. When I first began putting pen to paper, I thought I was capturing these moments in time to leave for my daughter. I didn't realize that at the same time, I was reclaiming my voice and sense of self as well. For me it was important to share that despite challenges with life-changing events that happen, there is still human connection. It is connection that I personally believe can get us through and help create positive energy out in the world.

I share these stories not because they are rare, but because they are very human and real. Somewhere, there is someone carrying their own personal stories of cancer survival. If these pages can offer even one person the opportunity to share, then I have completed my goal.

Life takes us on some wild twists and turns. I have found, for me, the key is to focus on removing toxicity and to spread positivity. At the end of each story, I posed questions to hopefully encourage ongoing thoughts and to offer different ways to share connection and positivity in our world.

After all is said and done, I asked myself what I wanted my legacy to be. I sat and meditated on this. After long and deep contemplation, I found that I want to be an example for my daughter. I want her to see that resilience is true beauty and to understand the power of human connection and love. I want to contribute to better outcomes in my community and world. I hope to create philanthropy and help support those to find their voice and inner strength after cancer.

I leave you with these final questions.

Will you be able to use any components of these stories or questions to help lift up someone in your life...or even someone you have never met? What do you want your legacy to be?

From the bottom of my heart, I thank you for allowing me
this time to share these stories with you.
It was Human Connection that brought us together.

Acknowledgements

I would like to acknowledge the following people and places, for all the love I received and for lifting me up: Gary, Sarah, Zoe, The Nunnies, Aunt Charlotte, Denise, Yoli, Jean, Grenda, Linda, The Calderone family, The Roth family, Shelly, Iren, Tannie, Lisa, Esperanza, Eli-59, Susan, Heidi, Lisa, Dr. Sharma, all my incredible Surgeons/Care Teams, Hailey, Phuong, Araceli, David G., Bob, Monica, Joe & Moni, Marta, Denise, Cabin 6, Delia, Dr. Fertal, Sifu Joseph Jackson, Khanhi, Linda V., Luz, Margie, Laura B., Sister T., Susan F., Kathie, Dee, Karyl, Lil-y, Lisa, My professor, Susan S., Anastasia, My incredible work teams, Vance, my YLO 45 family, San Juan Capistrano Mission, Niagara Falls, the LA Arboretum, Stearns Wharf, Ooltewah, The Charles River, St. Peregrine, St. Joseph, St. Jude
Cancer Kinship, Healing Odessey, Camp Kesem,
The trees that I would spend so much time with in meditation.
These powerful songs that carried me through:
"Gonna Fly Now" – Bill Conti
"I Got A Name" – Jim Croce
"This Is the Day"- The The
"This Must Be the Place (Naïve Melody)" - The Talking Heads

I am grateful for God's Loving Grace.

To all my TEAL SISTERS around the world, you are always in my heart and remember,
WE ARE TEAL STRONG.

Cover Photography by: Bob Rebholz
Thank you Bob for your vision and heart.

I would like to thank the following people for supporting me in this book journey.

Gary & Sarah for your love and helping me stay strong.

The Nunnies, your love and care truly lifted us up.

Shelly for encouraging me not to give up and Aunt Charlotte for believing in me from the very start.

Lisa and Joseph for inspiring me to look at the bigger picture.

Grenda and Linda for the prayers, love, and laughs.

Dan an incredible editor who helped me share my voice.

Jean for giving me the *"Spirit"* and encouragement to do this project when I doubted myself.

Lastly, I would like to thank you, the reader, for reading along my journey with me. Thank you for allowing me this time.

~

If you would kindly leave a review on Amazon for this book, it would be greatly welcomed. As a way to give back for all the support we received as a family, a portion of the proceeds from this book will go to support cancer support groups.

Many blessings to you all,
Tina

ABOUT THE AUTHOR

Tina Calderone Roth is a loving mother and wife. She resides in California and is deeply committed to serving her community. As a social worker, she is dedicated both professionally & personally to advocating for individuals and families who need guidance, resources, and to be heard. Her work is driven by a strong sense of values, compassion and empathy. She is rooted in equity, empowerment, and the importance of human connection. In her spare time, Tina volunteers in the community with several organizations and charities. She enjoys quilting, and repurposing old furniture. She also enjoys art, music, travelling and learning about new cultures.

If you would like to follow Tina's journey, you are welcome to follow her at www.Wherefearmeetsfaith.com or on the following social media platforms.

Facebook: Tina Calderone-Roth Where Fear Meets Faith.

Instagram: Wherefearmeetsfaith

www.ingramcontent.com/pod-product-compliance
Lightning Source LLC
LaVergne TN
LVHW090615110826
845146LV00001B/402

* 9 7 9 8 2 3 4 0 5 0 0 4 5 *